GREEN EDITION ®

At Dover Publications we're committed
earth-friendly manner and to helping our cus†

Manufacturing books in the United States ensures compliance with strict environmental laws and eliminates the need for international freight shipping, a major contributor to global air pollution. And printing on recycled paper helps minimize our consumption of trees, water and fossil fuels.

The text of this book was printed on paper made with 10% post-consumer waste and the cover was printed on paper made with 10% post-consumer waste. At Dover, we use Environmental Defense's Paper Calculator to measure the benefits of these choices, including: the number of trees saved, gallons of water conserved, as well as air emissions and solid waste eliminated.

Courier Corporation, the manufacturer of this book, owns the Green Edition Trademark.

Please visit the product page for *Chinese Clip Art for Machine Embroidery* at www.doverpublications.com to see a detailed account of the environmental savings we've achieved over the life of this book.

CHINESE CLIP ART
FOR MACHINE EMBROIDERY

Manufactured in the United States by Courier Corporation
99160101
www.doverpublications.com

Chinese Clip Art for Machine Embroidery

In this book you will find a collection of rare, authentic Chinese designs. These images have been carefully chosen, cleaned and prepped to give you the best quality images to use with your electronic embroidery design-making software. This unique publication helps you skip the time-consuming scanning and cleaning of images, and let's you jump right to the fun part—pattern making and sewing out!

What's in the book:

The book is a visual index of all of the files that are on the accompanying CD. In the upper left or right hand corner of each index page are the image numbers that correspond to the equivalent files on the CD.

For every image there are different color ideas for each design.

Next to each color idea is a list of the colors that are used in the design. The number refers to the Isacord thread color number.

The black-and-white version shows the file that you can use in your design-making program, to create the sewable pattern.

075, 076

4030	
1106	
0221	

5610	5100
5940	5050
0610	1114

0702	
0704	
1300	

1335	5100
5912	5940
4240	0706

17

On the inside covers of this book you will find a thread conversion chart, which helps you choose the appropriate thread color from four different manufacturers.

2

What's on the CD:

The outline versions of the images can be used with many design-making programs to create sewable patterns. Consult your program's instruction manual for specific instructions. There are both JPG and vector versions of these images on the CD.

The mass versions of the images can be used with most design-making programs to create sewable patterns. There are JPG and vector versions on the CD.

There are multiple color versions of each design on the CD. In addition to using them as a source for color ideas, these JPG images can be used as clip art for any crafts or graphics project. These files are located in the "Color JPG" folder.

Here is a finished, sewn-out pattern that was made using Brother's PE Design® software program, and Dover clip art.

6051	
3810	
0590	
1302	

3845	
5515	
1306	
5610	

1532	
3103	
1060	
3262	

1106	
0625	
5832	

5600	
3340	
3430	

5515	
0620	
3211	

1306
5610
0625

5415
3840
3901

0800
1099
1335

3543
3750
5210

0625
1725
1705

0551
0532
6156

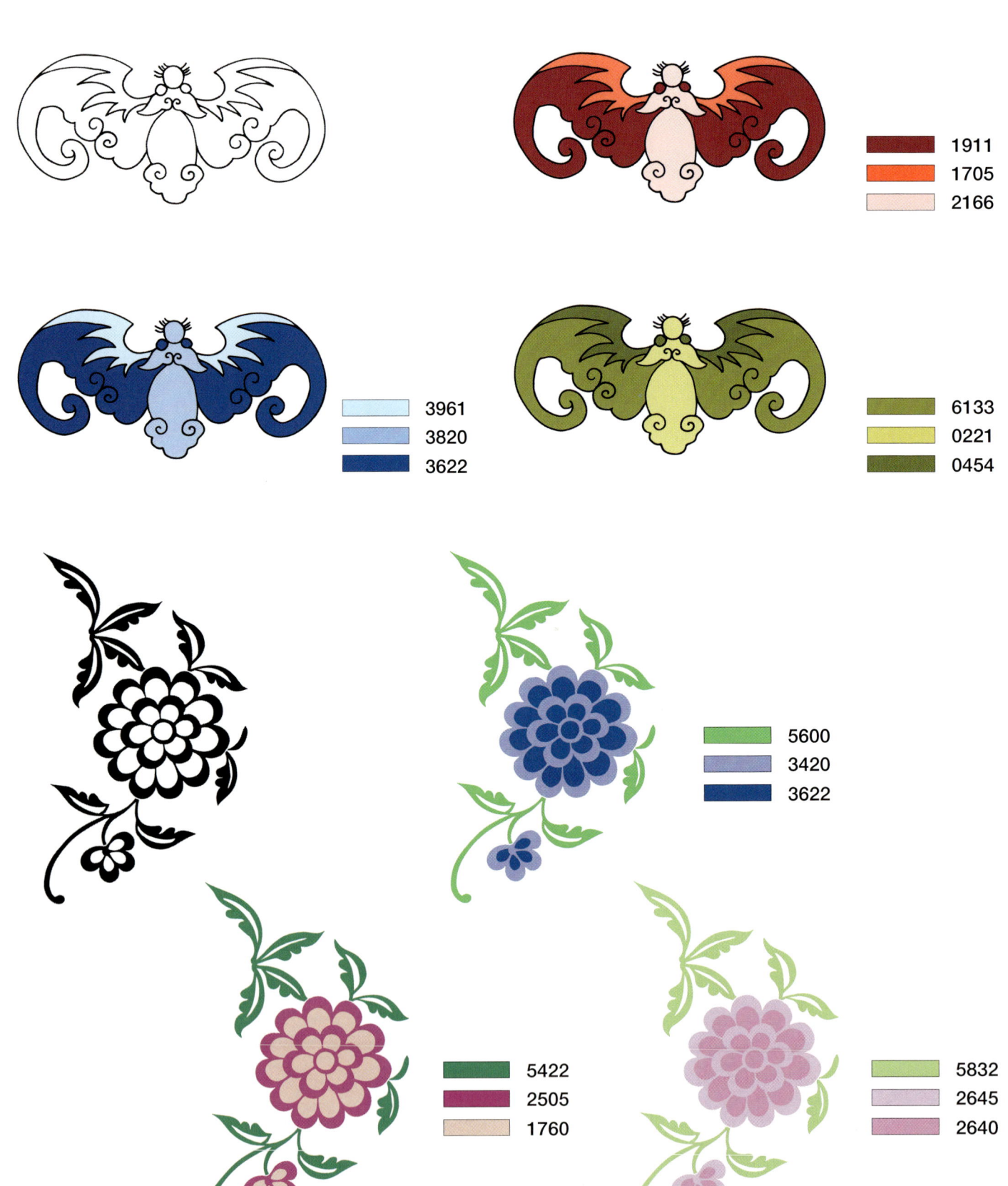

1911
1705
2166

3961
3820
3622

6133
0221
0454

5600
3420
3622

5422
2505
1760

5832
2645
2640

	5832			0532
	5633			0551
	1913			0830

	3211			4625
	2655			0713
	5610			4440
	5510			1300

	1324			4432
	5822			5050
	5020			0822
	1705			5840

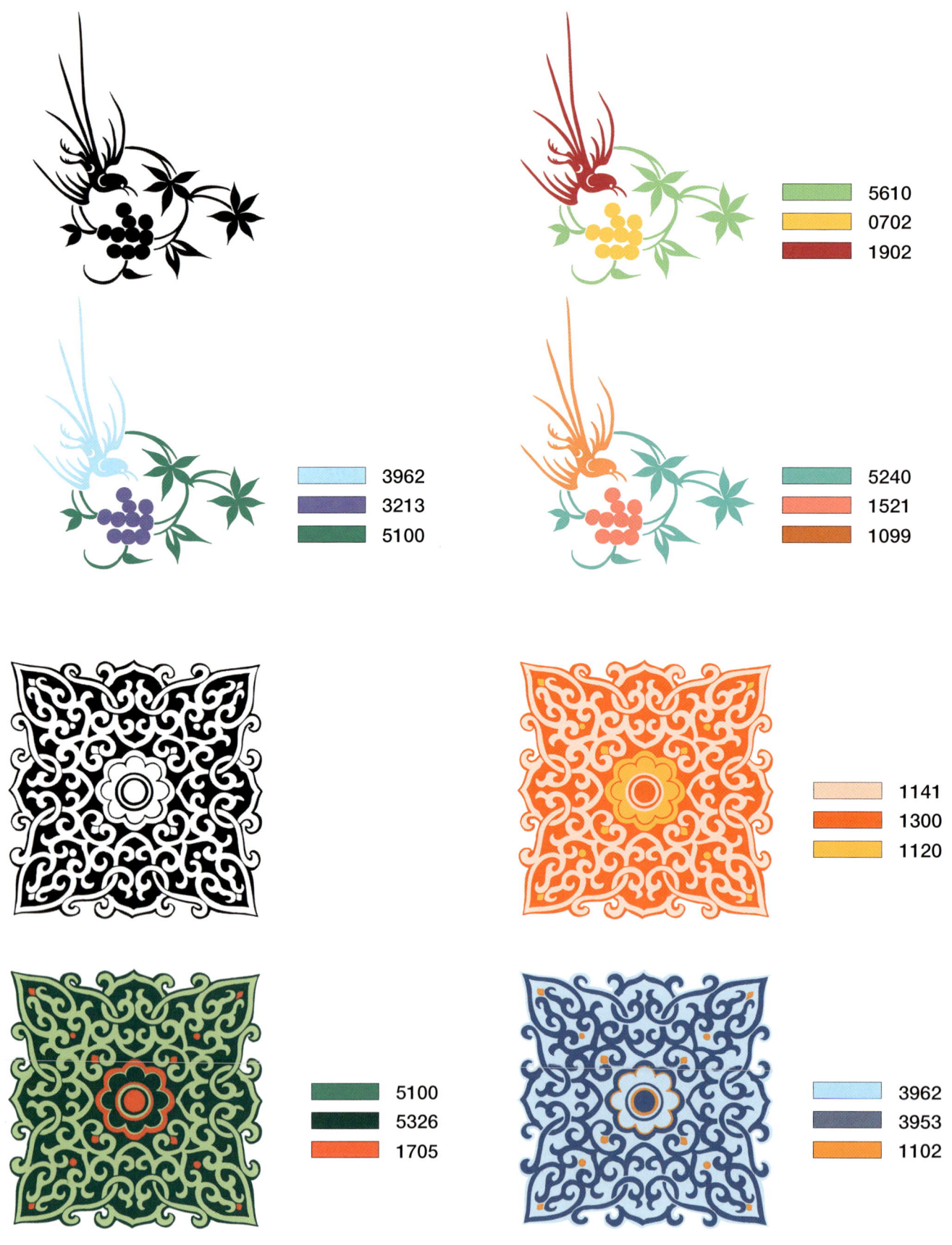

5610
0702
1902

3962
3213
5100

5240
1521
1099

1141
1300
1120

5100
5326
1705

3962
3953
1102

5513		5840	
1840		4440	
1849		4531	

2645		5934	
5912		5940	
5633		0830	
2504		0713	

0520		0900	
0506		0620	
0454		5600	

5010	
5912	
5324	

5832	
1501	
1106	

1120	
1304	
1342	

5324	
5940	
0615	
0702	

1302	
1141	
5610	
5411	

3262	
2920	
0726	
0221	

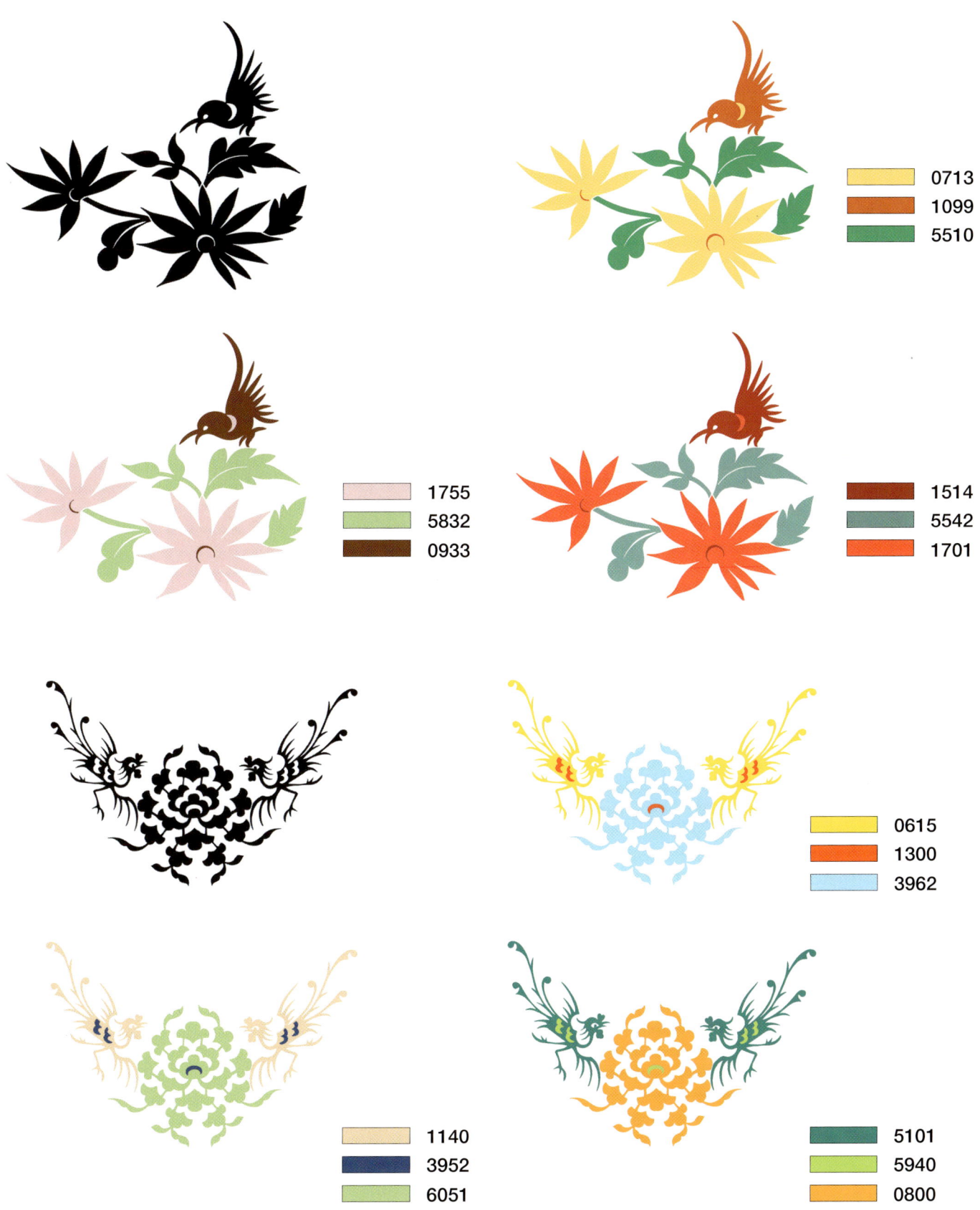

	0713
	1099
	5510

	1755
	5832
	0933

	1514
	5542
	1701

	0615
	1300
	3962

	1140
	3952
	6051

	5101
	5940
	0800

0605
5531
5010

1501
4840
5940

4030
1106
0221

5500
5513
1306

5610
5940
0610

3640
0822
0713

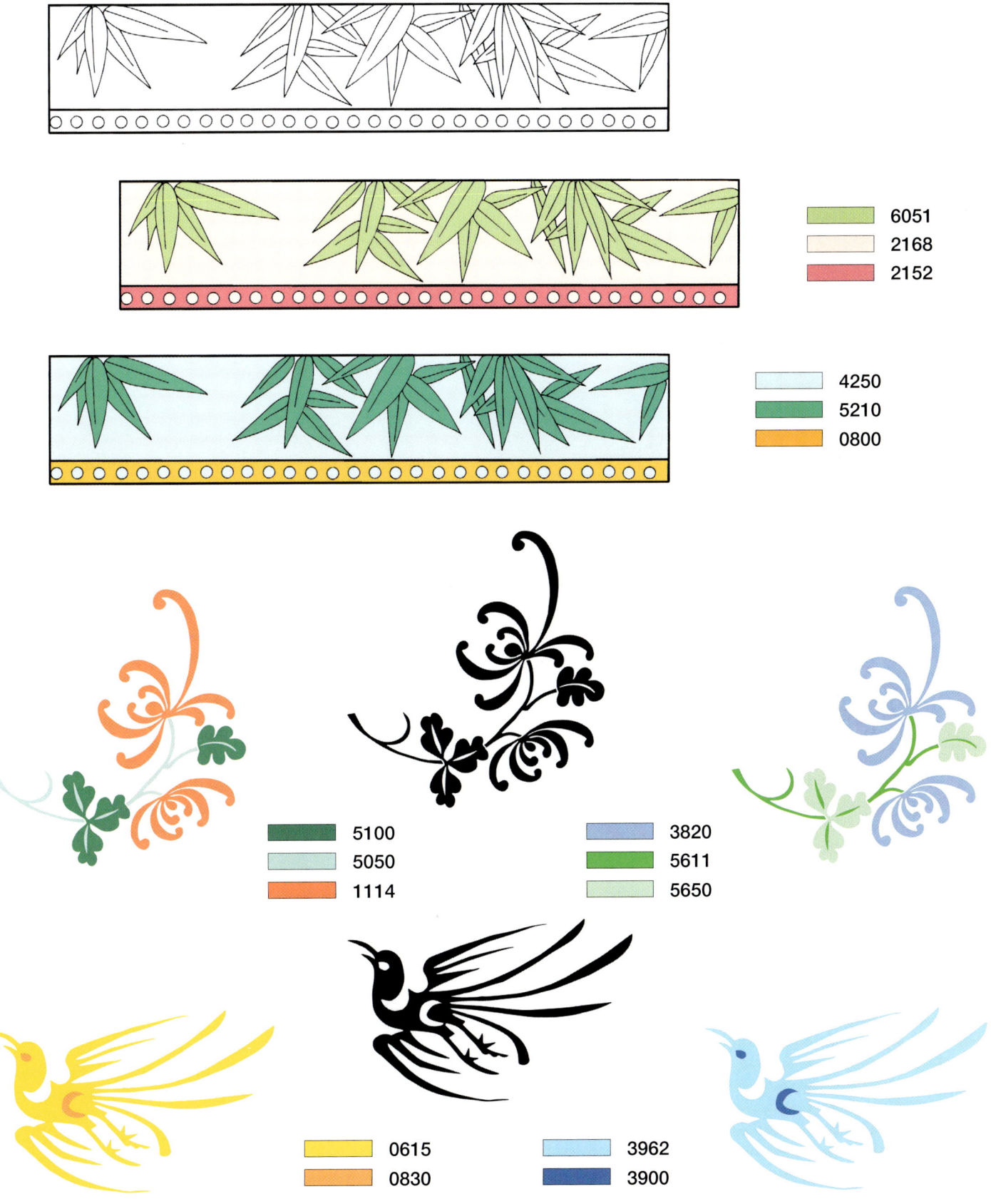

6051
2168
2152

4250
5210
0800

5100
5050
1114

3820
5611
5650

0615
0830

3962
3900

	5500
	1120
	4030

	1304
	0590
	0713

	0605
	3640
	5610

	3045
	0311
	0704
	2910

	0221
	0232
	5422
	5610

	2011
	1940
	5822
	5600

1300
0605
1914

5050
4240
0904

5620
5940
0506

2645
2524
2611

3901
4250
1421

0805
1305
4620

	3961
	5240
	3810

	0630
	0830
	5610

	5411
	5610
	1850

	0221
	0232
	3040

	0501
	0610

	3901
	3961

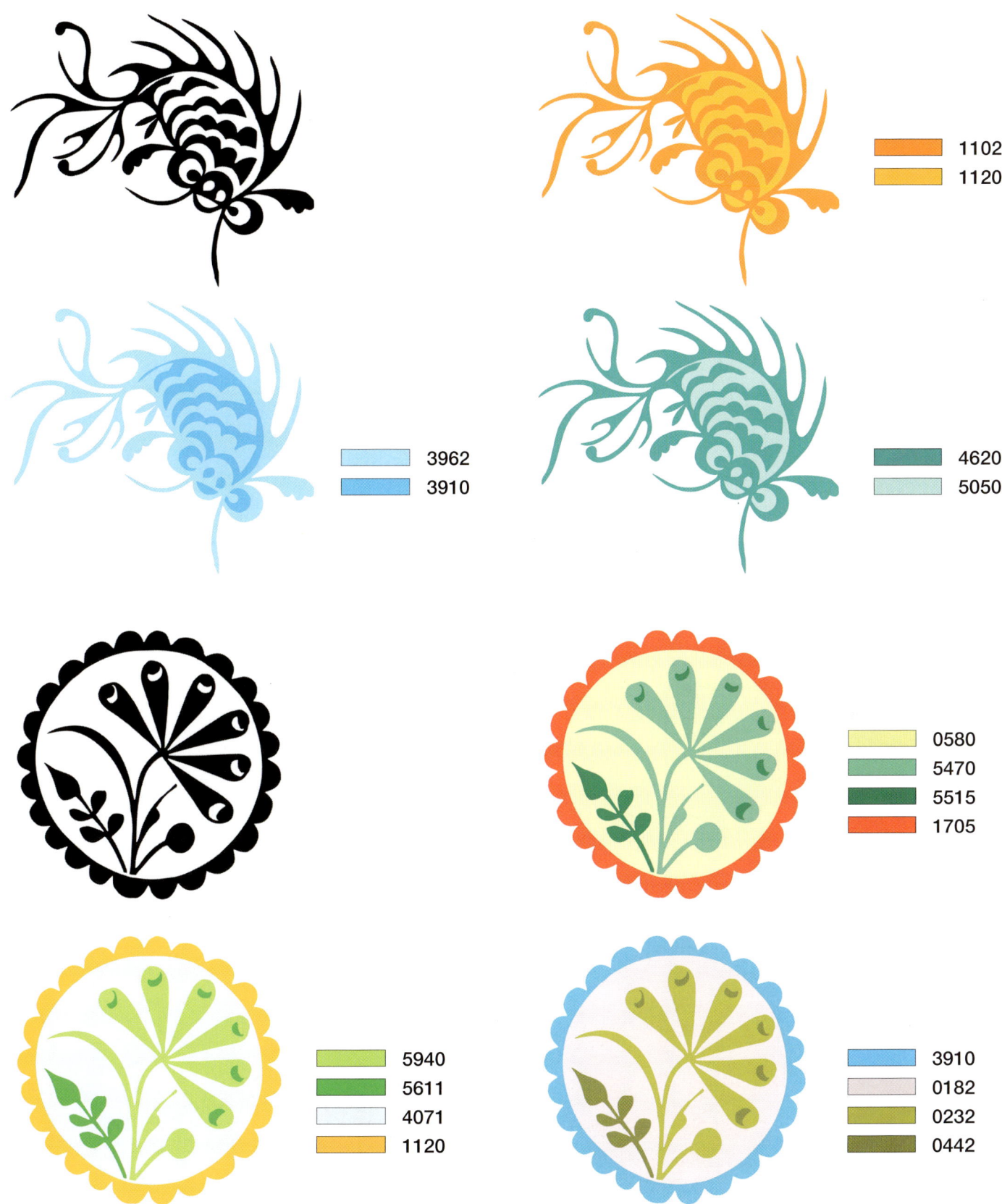

1102
1120

3962
3910

4620
5050

0580
5470
5515
1705

5940
5611
4071
1120

3910
0182
0232
0442

0702
0704
1300

1335
5912
4240

5100
5940
0706

4250
4022
0851
0933

5050
5633
1113
0532

3845
3251
3211
0250

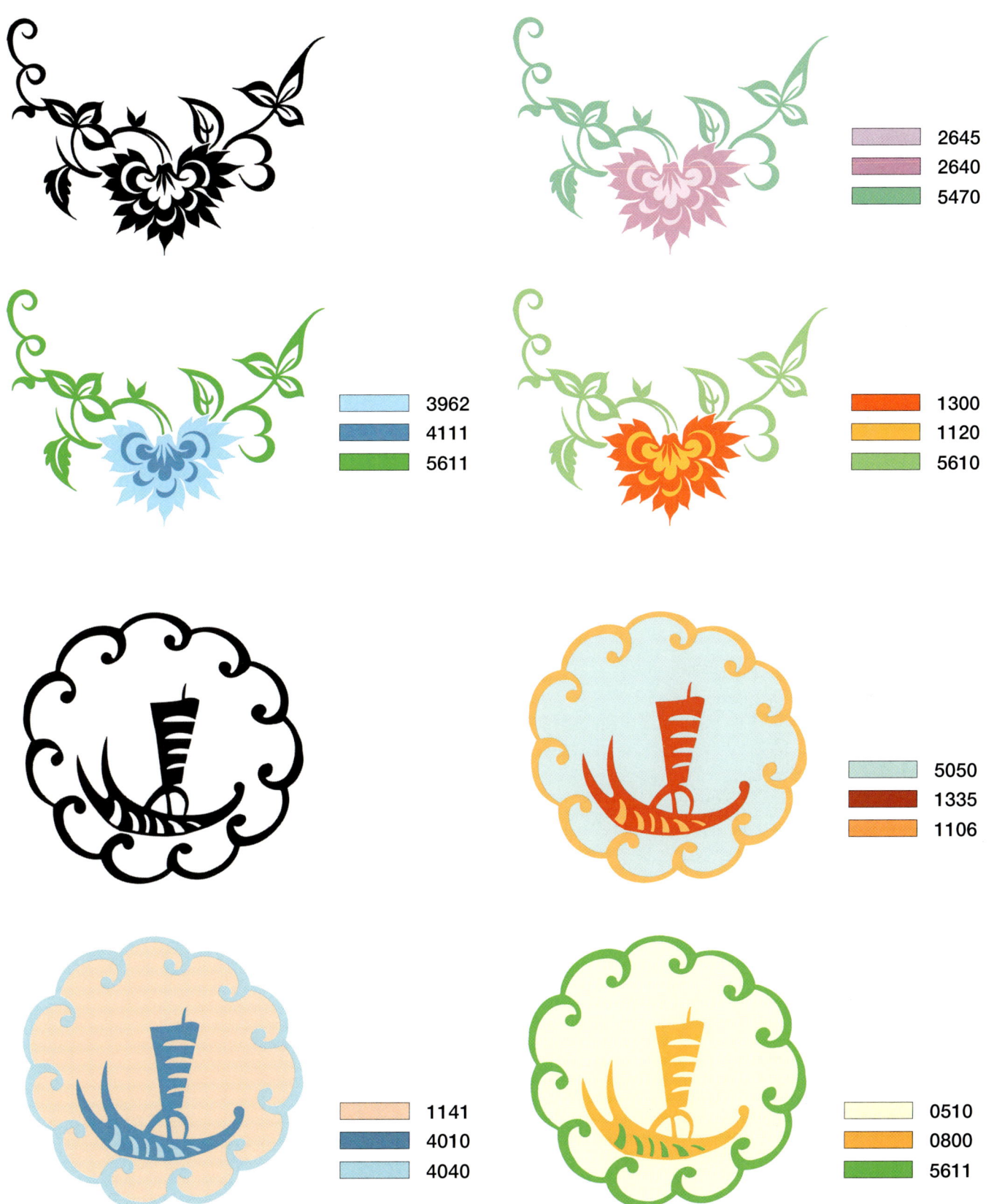

2645
2640
5470

3962
4111
5611

1300
1120
5610

5050
1335
1106

1141
4010
4040

0510
0800
5611

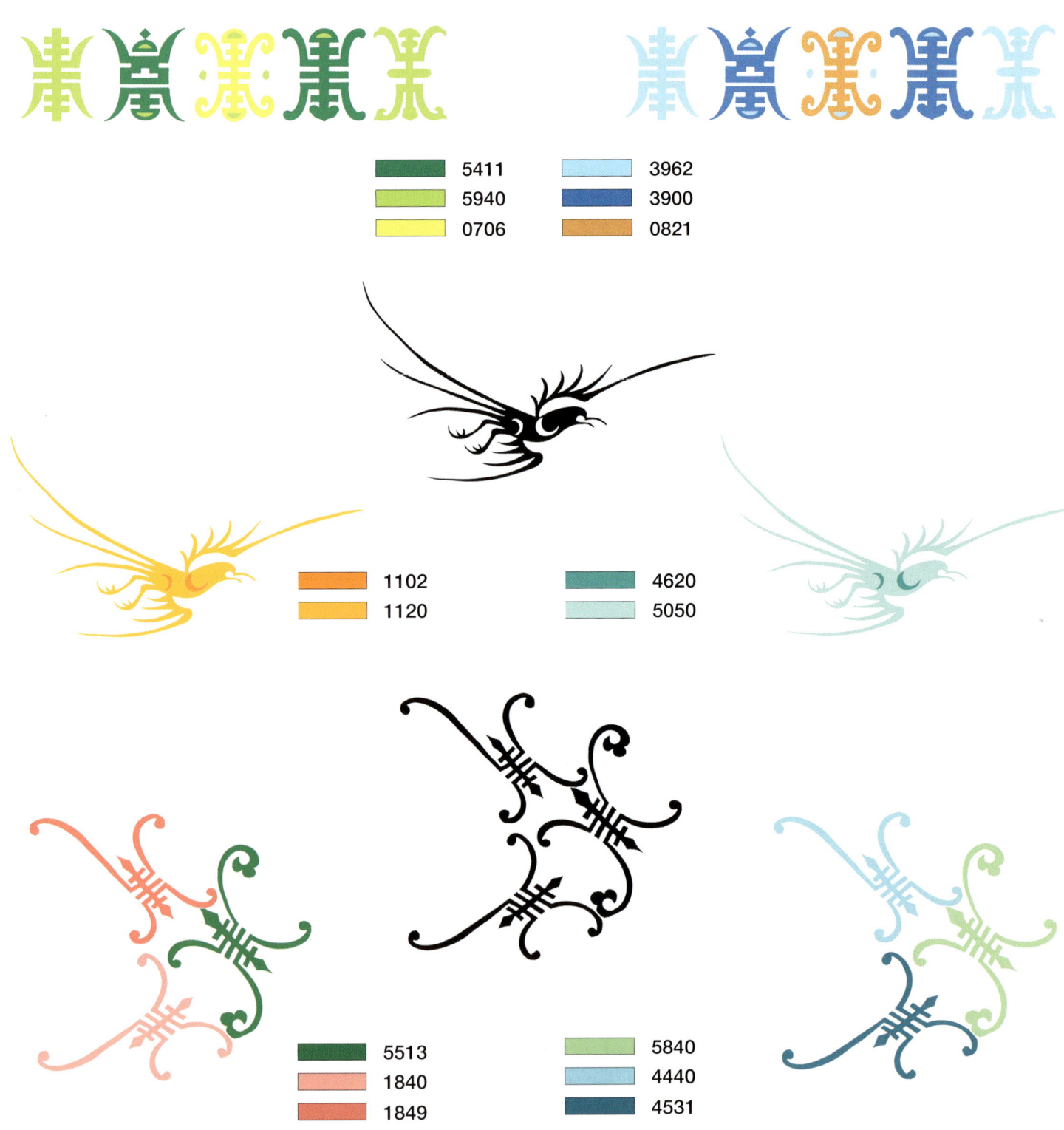

5411		3962		
5940		3900		
0706		0821		

1102		4620
1120		5050

5513		5840
1840		4440
1849		4531

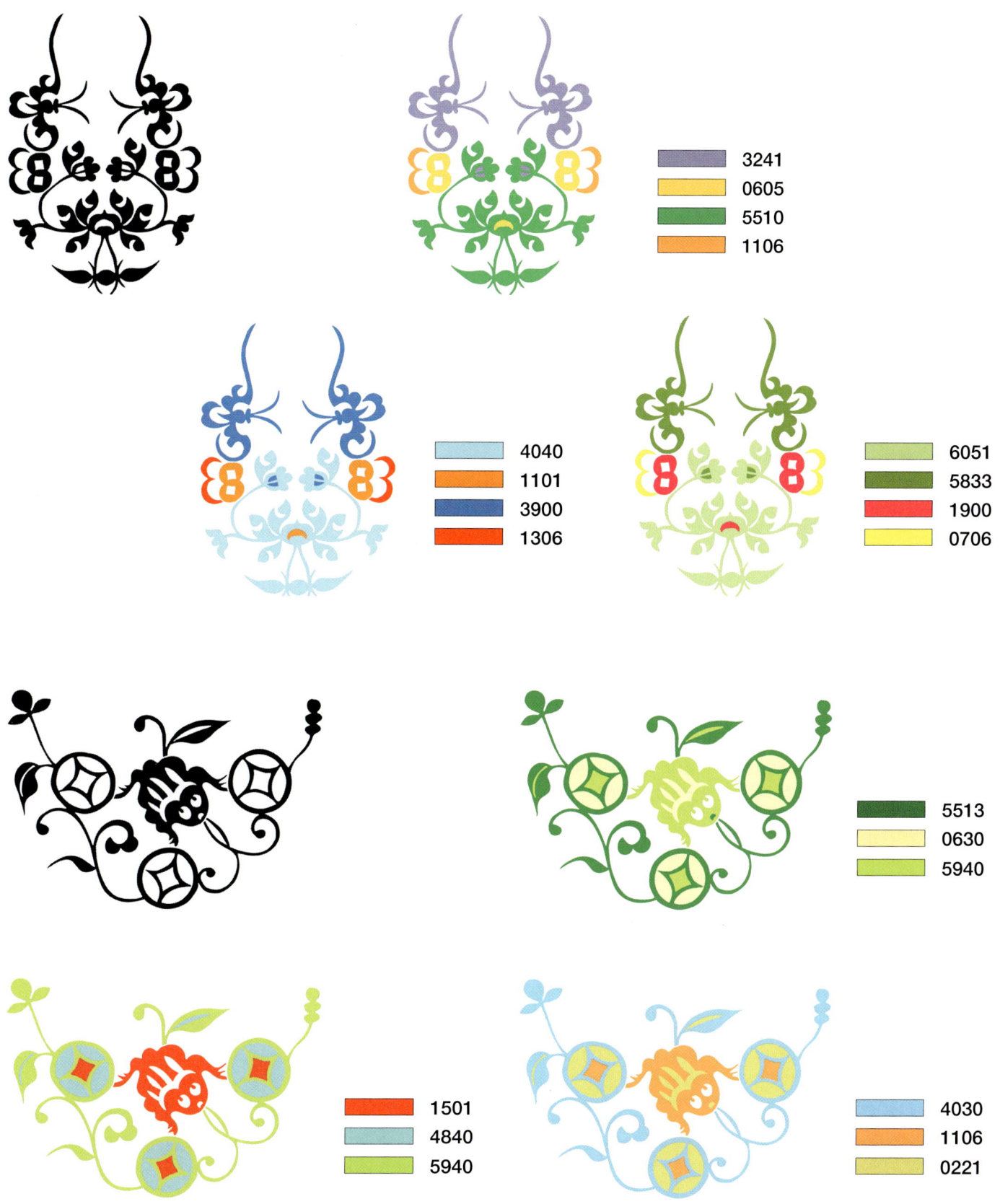

	3241
	0605
	5510
	1106

	4040
	1101
	3900
	1306

	6051
	5833
	1900
	0706

	5513
	0630
	5940

	1501
	4840
	5940

	4030
	1106
	0221

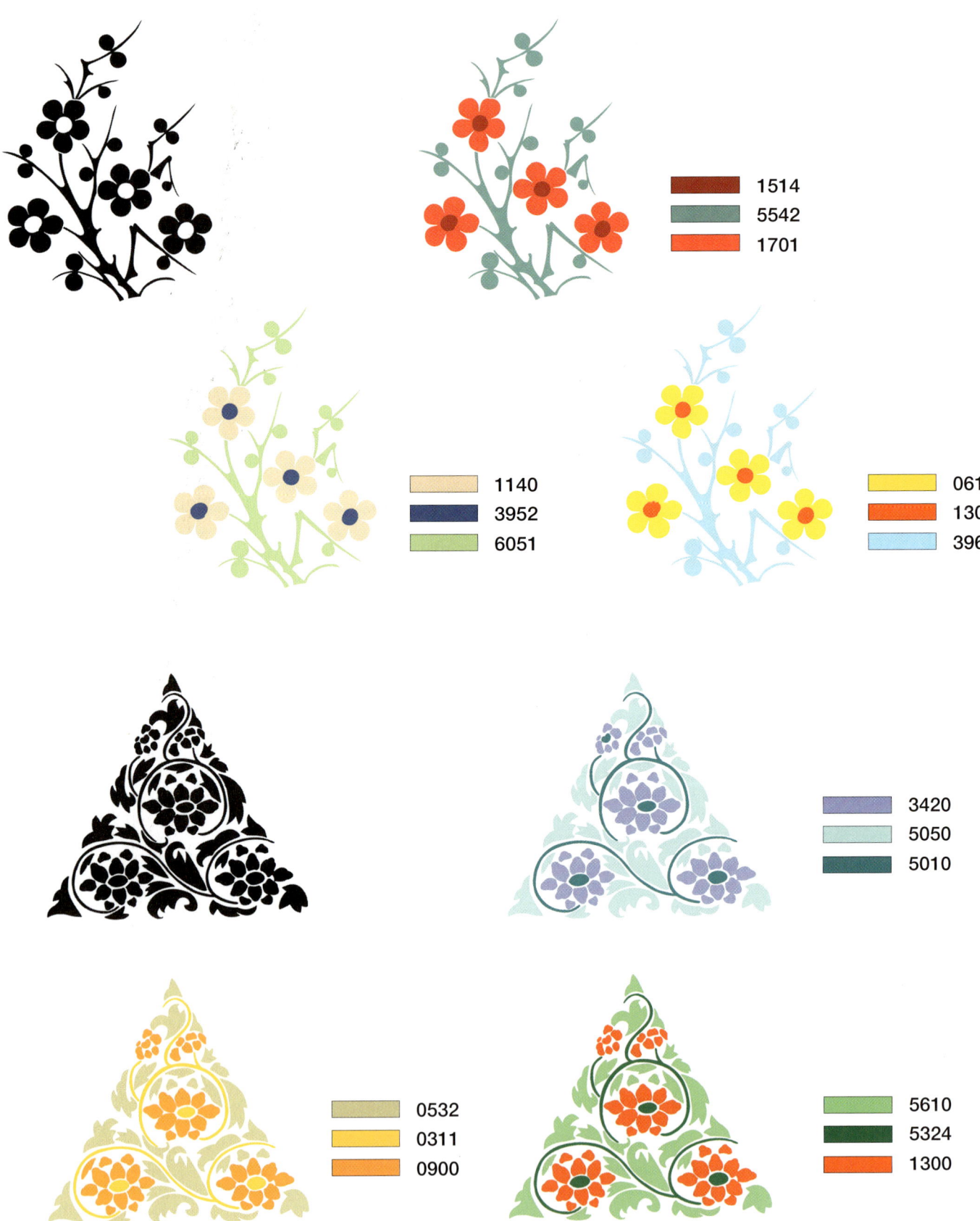

1514
5542
1701

1140
3952
6051

0615
1300
3962

3420
5050
5010

0532
0311
0900

5610
5324
1300

	5230		1106
	5650		1306
	1120		5840
	4410		

	5940		4010
	5513		4250
	1902		1123
	0713		1101

	1940		0610
	1800		3213
	5470		5840

5610
0702
1902

3962
3213
5100

5240
1521
1099

3262
2920
0726
0221

5324
5940
0615
0702

1302
1141
5610
5411

| | 3543 |
| | 3750 |

| | 0625 |
| | 1725 |

| | 0551 |
| | 0532 |

	0702
	0704
	1300

	1335
	5912
	4240

	5100
	5940
	0706

	6051
	5940
	1705i

	5610
	5940
	0610

	5100
	5050
	1114

	3820
	5611
	5650

	4250
	5210
	0800

	6051
	2168
	2152

■ 3910	
■ 0182	
■ 0232	
■ 0442	

■ 5940	
■ 5611	
■ 3961	
■ 1120	

■ 0580	
■ 5470	
■ 5515	
■ 1705	

■ 4040	
■ 1101	
■ 3900	
■ 1306	

■ 3241	
■ 0605	
■ 5510	
■ 1106	

■ 6051	
■ 5833	
■ 1900	
■ 0706	

	1106		5600
	0625		3340
	5832		3430

	1755		0713
	5832		1099
	1860		5510

	5050		0510
	5230		0800
	0610		5611

6051
5833
1900
0706

3340
0605
5510
1106

4040
1101
3900
1306

2645
5912
5633

3962
3953
1102

5610
0702
1902

	0501
	0610

	4620
	5050

	3901
	3961

	5940
	5513
	1902
	0713

	4010
	4250
	1123
	1101

	5230
	5650
	1120
	4410

2645
2640
5470

5100
5940
0706

3962
4111
5611

5610
5411

1302
1141

1102
1120

3962
3213
5650

5240
1521
1099

5610
0702
1902

0610
3213
5840

0532
0311
0900

5610
5324
1300

	5411
	5610
	1850

	0221
	0232
	3040

	3420
	3650
	5010

	5650
	4440
	4531

	5415
	3840
	3901

	1306
	5610
	0625

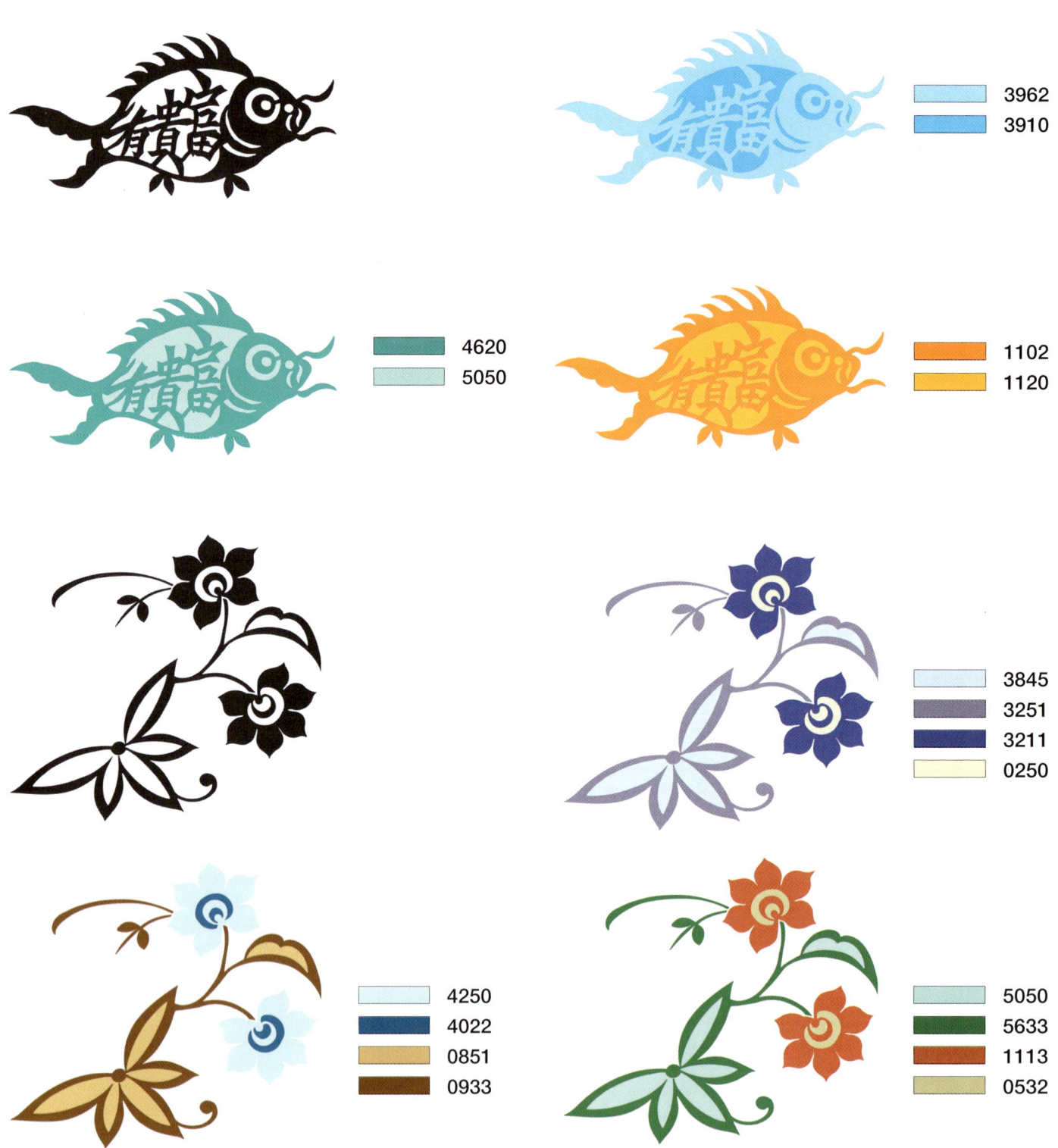

	3962
	3910

	4620
	5050

	1102
	1120

	3845
	3251
	3211
	0250

	4250
	4022
	0851
	0933

	5050
	5633
	1113
	0532

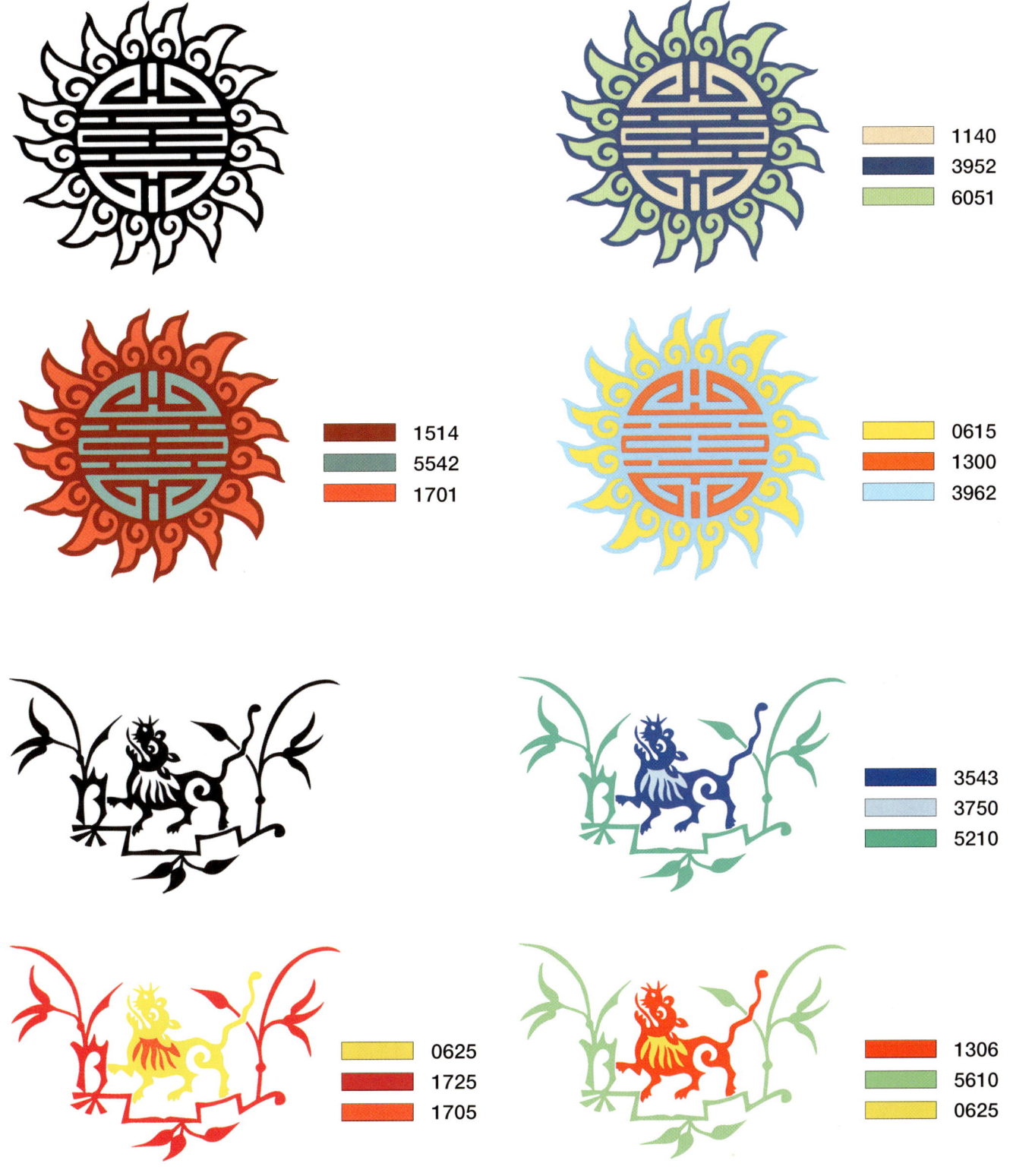

	1140
	3952
	6051

	1514
	5542
	1701

	0615
	1300
	3962

	3543
	3750
	5210

	0625
	1725
	1705

	1306
	5610
	0625

	5610
	5324
	1300

	0532
	0311
	0900

	3420
	5050
	5010

	5050
	1335
	1106

	1141
	4010
	4040

	0510
	0800
	5611

4030
1106
0221

5610
5940
0610

5100
5050
1114

0702
0704
1300

1335
5912
4240

5100
5940
0706

3262
2920
0726
0221

1302
1141
5610
5411

5324
5940
0615
0702

1102
1120

1302
1141

5610
5411

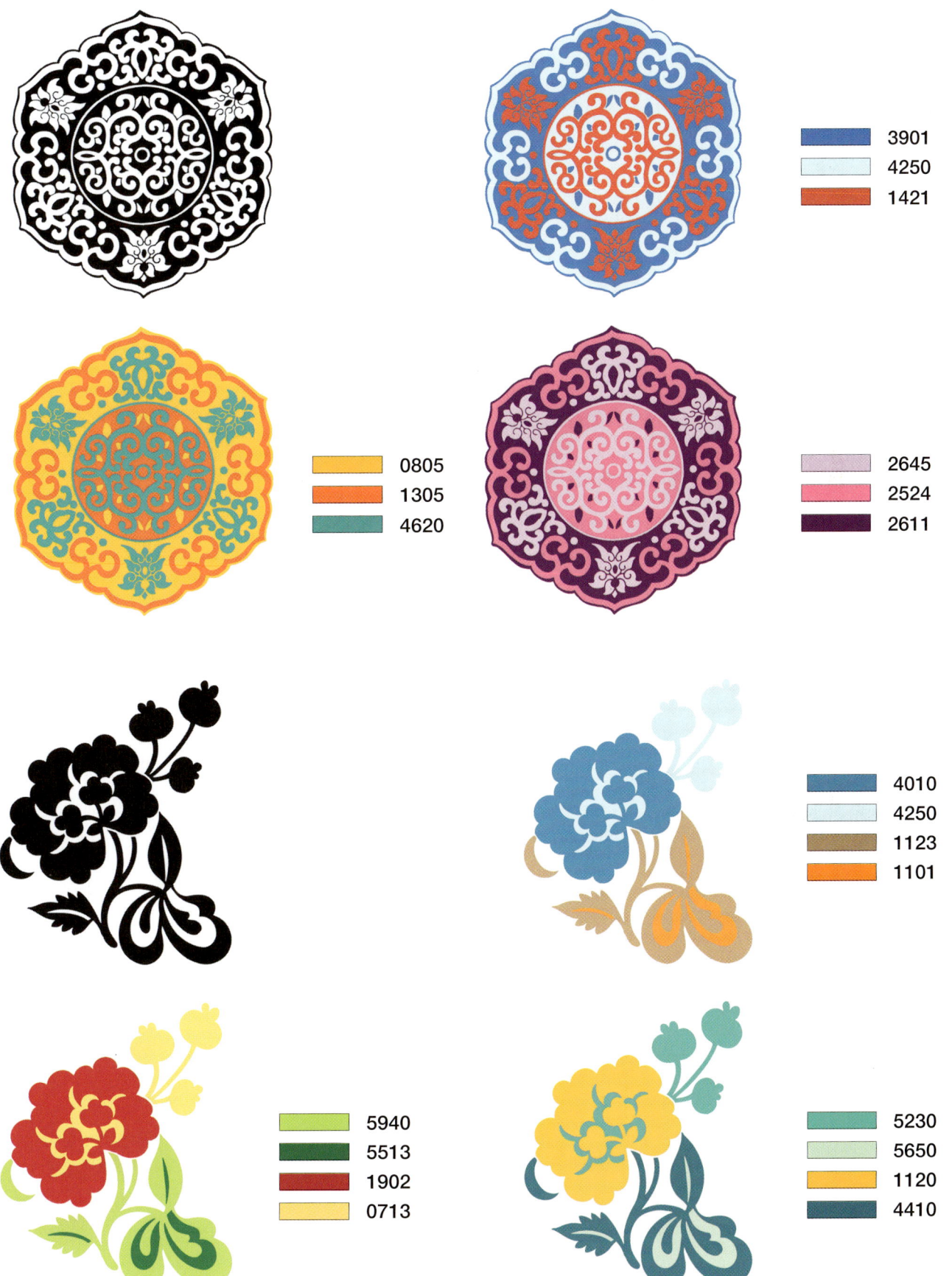

3901
4250
1421

0805
1305
4620

2645
2524
2611

4010
4250
1123
1101

5940
5513
1902
0713

5230
5650
1120
4410

	3211
	2655
	5610
	5510

	4625
	0713
	4440
	1300

	1324
	5822
	5020
	1705

	0501
	0610

	3901
	3961

	5610
	1850

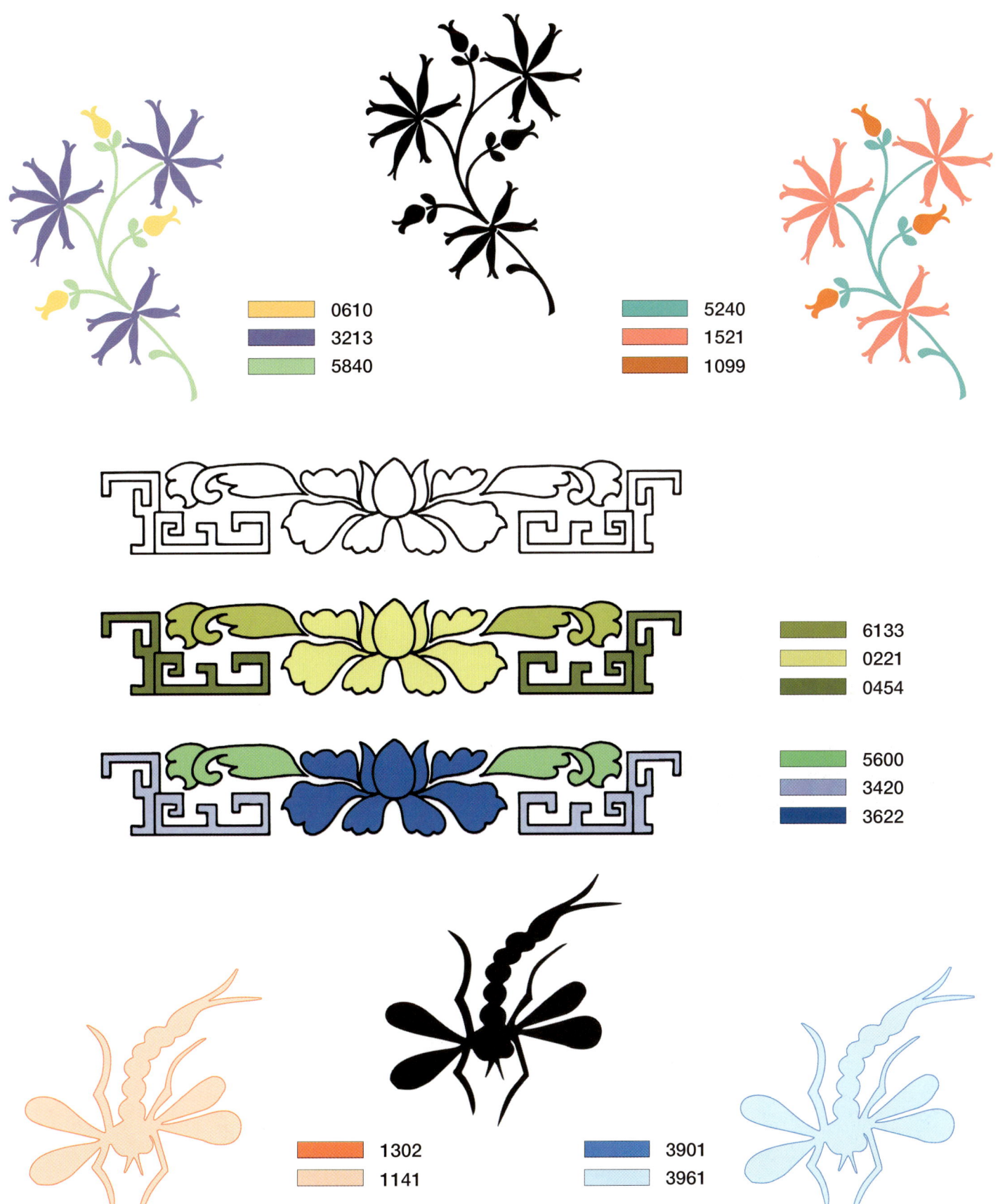

0610
3213
5840

5240
1521
1099

6133
0221
0454

5600
3420
3622

1302
1141

3901
3961

	4010
	4250
	1123
	1101

	5050
	5633
	1113
	0532

	5940
	5611
	3961
	1120

	3910
	0182
	0232
	0442

	4040
	1101
	3900
	1352

	0580
	5470
	5515
	1705

	1102
	1120

	4620
	5050

	3901
	3961

	6051
	5833
	1900
	0706

	3241
	0605
	5510
	1106

	5324
	5940
	0615
	0702

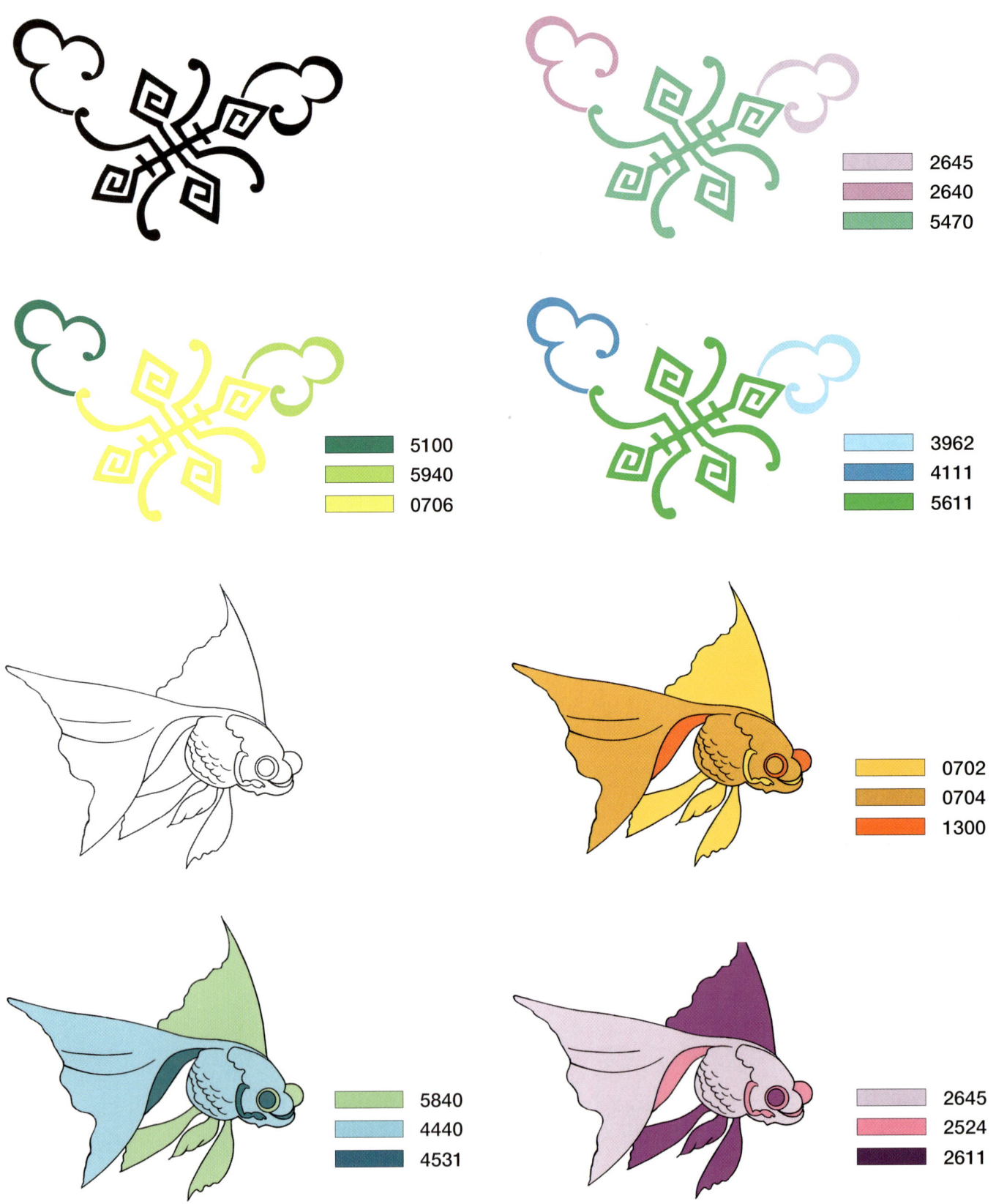

	2645
	2640
	5470

	5100
	5940
	0706

	3962
	4111
	5611

	0702
	0704
	1300

	5840
	4440
	4531

	2645
	2524
	2611

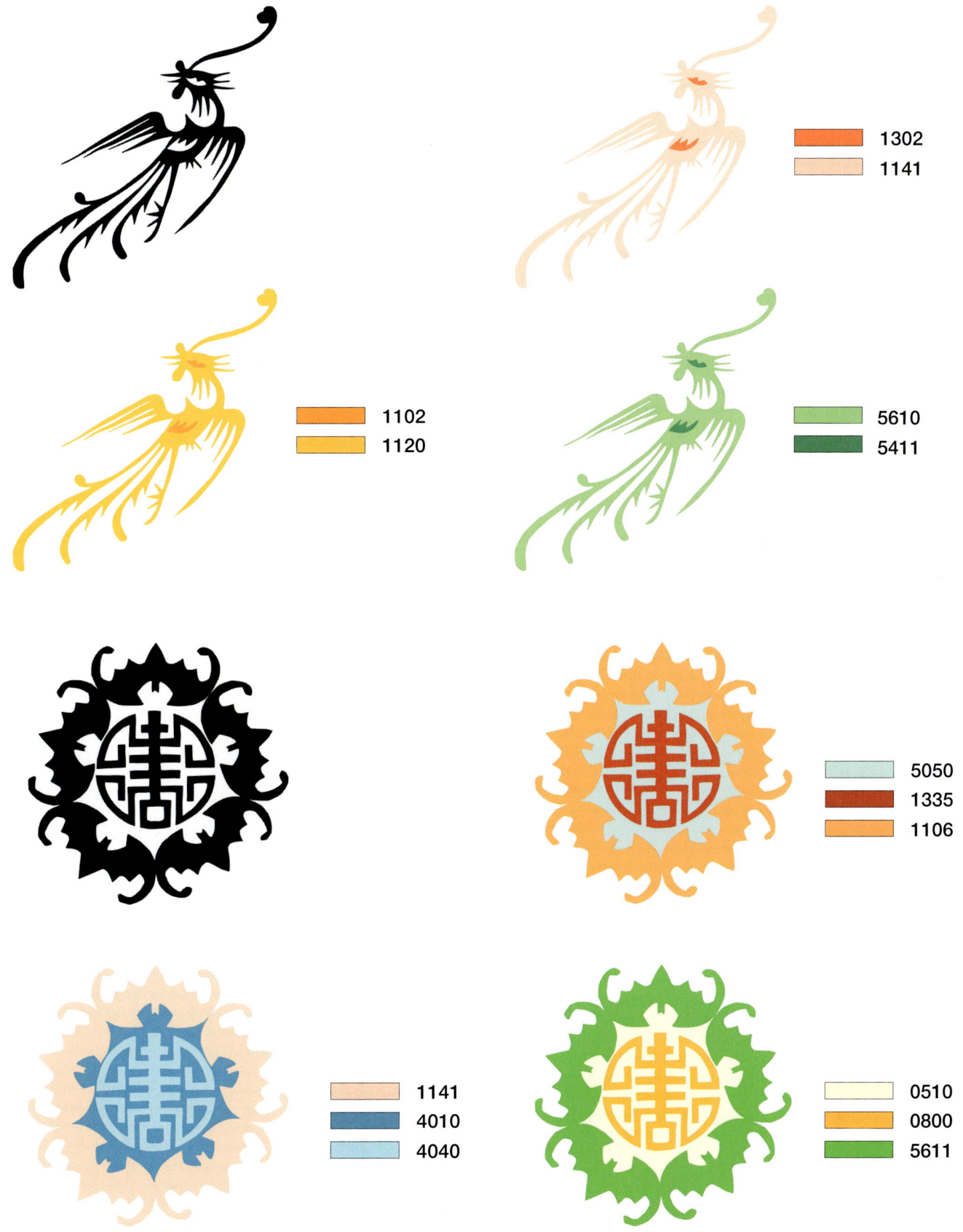

1302
1141

1102
1120

5610
5411

5050
1335
1106

1141
4010
4040

0510
0800
5611

3543
3750

0625
1725

0551
0532

1300
0605
1914

5050
4240
0904

5620
5940
0506

0610
3213
5840

1106
1306
5840

1940
1800
5470

3420
5050
5010

4620
5050

1102
1120

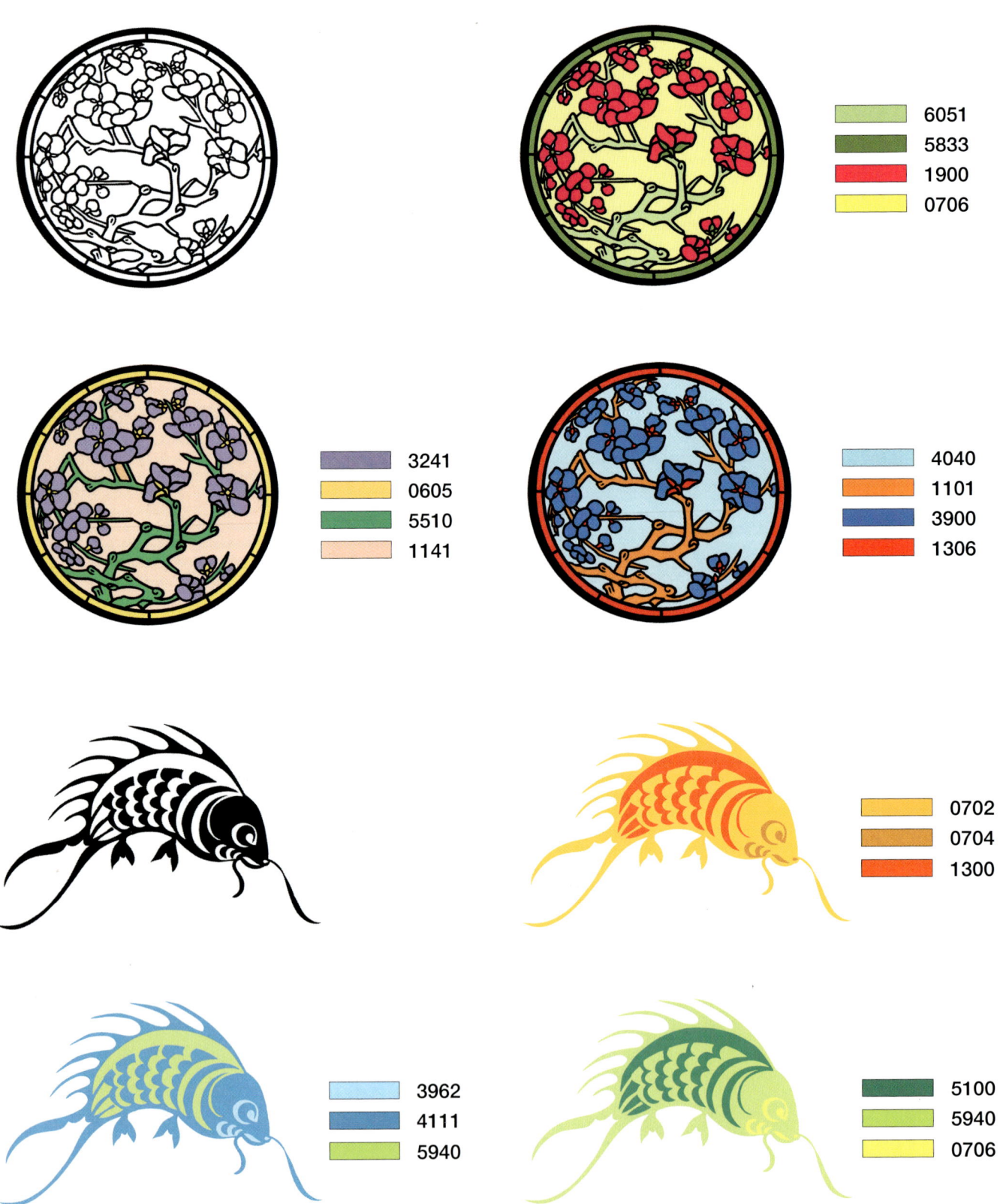

	6051
	5833
	1900
	0706

	3241
	0605
	5510
	1141

	4040
	1101
	3900
	1306

	0702
	0704
	1300

	3962
	4111
	5940

	5100
	5940
	0706